Focus on Steroids

Focus on Steroids

A Drug-Alert Book

Katherine S. Talmadge
Illustrated by David Neuhaus

Twenty-First Century Books

A Division of Henry Holt and Co., Inc.

Frederick, Maryland

Published by
Twenty-First Century Books
A Division of Henry Holt and Co., Inc.
38 South Market Street
Frederick, Maryland 21701

Printed in the United States of America

10   9   8   7   6   5   4   3   2

Library of Congress Cataloging in Publication Data

Talmadge, Katherine S.
Focus on Steroids
Illustrated by David Neuhaus

(A Drug-Alert Book)
Summary: Examines steroids, with an emphasis
on anabolic steroids, discussing their effects on the body,
danges, and use in sports.
1. Doping in sports—Juvenile literature.
2. Anabolic steroids—Health aspects—Juvenile literature.
[1. Anabolic steroids.   2. Steroids.   3. Drugs.
4. Drug Abuse.   5. Doping in sports.]
I. Neuhaus, David, ill.   II. Title.
III. Series: The Drug-Alert Series.
RC1230.T35   1991
362.29'088796—dc20   90-40584   CIP   AC
ISBN 0-8050-2216-3

Table of Contents

Introduction

"Baby Saved by Miracle Drug!" "Drug Bust at Local School!" Headlines like these are often side by side in your newspaper, or you may hear them on the evening news. This is confusing. If drugs save lives, why are people arrested for having and selling them?

The word "drug" is part of the confusion. It is a word with many meanings. The drug that saves a baby's life is also called a medicine. The illegal drugs found at the local school have many names—names like pot, speed, and crack. But one name for all of these illegal drugs is dope.

Some medicines you can buy at your local drugstore or grocery store, and there are other medicines only a doctor can get for you. But whether you buy them yourself or need a doctor to order them for you, medicines are made to get you healthy when you are sick.

Dope is not for sale in any store. You can't get it from a doctor. Dope is bought from someone called a "dealer" or a "pusher" because using, buying, or selling dope is against the law. That doesn't stop some people from using dope. They say they do it to change the way they feel. Often, that means they are trying to run away from their problems. But when the dope wears off, the problems are still there—and they are often worse than before.

There are three drugs we see so often that we sometimes forget they really are drugs. These are alcohol, nicotine, and caffeine. Alcohol is in beer, wine, and liquor. Nicotine is found in cigarettes, cigars, pipe tobacco, and other tobacco products. Caffeine is in coffee, tea, soft drinks, and chocolate. These three drugs are legal. They are sold in stores. But that doesn't mean they are always safe to use. Alcohol and nicotine are such strong drugs that only adults are allowed to buy and use them. And most parents try to keep their children from having too much caffeine.

Marijuana, cocaine, alcohol, nicotine, caffeine, medicines: these are all drugs. All drugs are alike because they change the way our bodies and minds work. But different drugs cause different changes. Some help, and some harm. And when they aren't used properly, even helpful drugs can harm us.

Figuring all this out is not easy. That's why The Drug-Alert Books were written: so you will know why certain drugs are used, how they affect people, why they are dangerous, and what laws there are to control them.

Knowing about drugs is important. It is important to you and to all the people who care about you.

David Friedman, Ph.D.
Consulting Editor

Dr. David Friedman is Associate Professor of Physiology and Pharmacology and Assistant Dean of Research Development at the Bowman Gray School of Medicine, Wake Forest University.

Winning and Losing
with Steroids

It's a bright September day in Seoul, Korea. From all over the world, people gather to watch today's big race.

The 1988 Olympic games are under way.

Down on the track, the runners are warming up. You can almost feel the excitement in the air. In just a few minutes, the blast of the starting gun will send the fastest men alive to victory or defeat. The 100-meter dash will begin!

You and a friend are watching the race on television. You can hardly sit still! For weeks, everyone at school has been waiting for this race. Everyone has been making predictions and quoting the sportswriters. For weeks, everyone has been waiting and wondering. Will Canadian runner Ben Johnson win? Will he slash time off the world record that he set himself in 1987? Or will Carl Lewis, the great American runner, win? Who will capture the Olympic gold medal, the highest honor in amateur sports? This is going to be a great race!

The runners take their starting positions. "Lewis is going to win this time," your friend says.

"I don't think so," you answer. "Today's Ben's day. I just know it."

Over the past eight years, Ben Johnson and Carl Lewis have run against each other 15 times. Lewis won nine of the races, and Johnson won six. But Johnson has won most of the recent races. In the course of these races, he set new world records—and then beat his own records! In 1987, Johnson set the world record for the 100-meter dash at 9.83 seconds.

The blast of the starting gun makes you jump from your chair. The runners are off!

"Come on, Ben!" you cheer. "Go for the gold!"

"Come on, Carl!" your friend roars. "Beat him!"

The Olympic drama is packed into less than ten seconds. You hold your breath. The runners go by in a blur. Johnson leads, but Lewis is practically breathing down his neck. As they cross the finish line, Johnson beats Lewis by one stride. He raises his hand to the sky, pointing his index finger to say, "I'm number one!" The time is 9.79. He has broken his own world record! He can claim the gold!

"Wow!" you shout. "Did you see Johnson tear that track apart? He left Lewis in the dust! I'd do *anything* to be able to run like that!"

Would you really do *anything*? There are lots of things you can do to make your body strong. You can eat healthy foods to strengthen your bones and build up your muscles. You can get regular exercise to feel and look fit. And to be a star on the athletic field, you can join a team and practice hard. You'll need to train every day. It will take lots of work.

Lots of hard work.

That's how Ben Johnson began his route to the Olympic gold medal. But Johnson made a mistake. He decided that he *would* do anything to win. He decided to use drugs.

After the race, he said, "I just wanted to beat Carl." Then, he climbed to the platform to accept the gold medal. People all over the world celebrated Johnson's astonishing victory and new world record.

Yet only two days later, the celebration came to an end. Traces of anabolic steroids were found in Johnson's urine. Anabolic steroids are drugs that some people use because they want to be bigger and stronger. They use anabolic steroids as a chemical short cut to a more muscular body. But it is a dangerous short cut and often leads to an unhappy end.

Like many other drugs, anabolic steroids change the way the body works. Like many other drugs, anabolic steroids also change the way the brain works. They change the way people think, feel, and act. And, like many other drugs, they can hurt both the body and the brain.

Athletes are warned over and over not to take anabolic steroids. In fact, in most sports leagues and competitions, it's against the rules.

But Ben Johnson broke the rules.

Why?

Why would such a great athlete take this kind of chance? Why would he risk getting caught? Why would he risk his health and life?

Because he felt tremendous pressure to be "the best." He felt that he *had* to win that race. He felt that he had to prove that he really was, as the sportswriters claimed, "the fastest human being alive." He thought that steroids would help him win. And, sadly, Ben Johnson isn't alone.

The pressure to win has led too many athletes—male and female—to take anabolic steroids. By using these drugs and working out, some athletes have become bigger and stronger than they would have become without steroids. Steroids help athletes to build strong muscles. They help athletes to recover quickly from training sessions, so they can work out more often. Steroids are a chemical short cut to a powerful body.

The pressure to be the best can be enormous on athletes, from the Olympic athlete running for the gold to the average high-school football player hoping to catch the eye of a college scout. But steroids are not just a problem for athletes. They are a problem for anyone who uses them.

And they are a special problem for young people today. One in every 15 male high-school seniors has used steroids. That's over 500,000 teenage steroid users.

Some boys in high school take steroids just to look big and strong. They feel unhappy with the way they look. They want to look like body builders. They use steroids to add size and strength to their muscles. Steroids can help them look bigger. Steroids can help them feel stronger.

But young people who use anabolic steroids are taking a terrible risk. They're risking a healthy body. They're risking a healthy life.

That's because steroids do more than just build muscles. They can destroy the body they are supposed to strengthen. They can cause heart disease, liver damage, and cancer. They can make a young person stop growing. They can also make people fly into sudden rages or become so deeply depressed that they may think about killing themselves.

That's why you and your friends need to know about steroids. This book will help you. It will tell you what steroids are and what they do to the body and the brain. It will tell you why people use steroids. And it will tell you why *not* to use steroids. It will give you the facts you need to say "No" to these dangerous drugs.

Ben Johnson wanted to be a winner. But he became a loser instead. Olympic officials took away the gold medal he won. They gave it to Carl Lewis, the man Johnson wanted so much to beat. Then, they erased from the record books his winning time of 9.79 seconds, as if it had never happened. Johnson also lost the world record he had set in 1987. Athletic officials found out that he had used steroids to win that race, too. He was suspended for two years from professional sports.

What happened to Ben Johnson is a terrible tragedy. He is a great athlete. He had a great future ahead of him. What happened to Ben Johnson is a lesson for other athletes who might think about using steroids. But what happened to Ben Johnson is not just a tragedy for the world of sports. It is not just a lesson for athletes.

It is a lesson for anyone who wants to be a winner.

What Are Anabolic Steroids?

A car is a powerful machine. Your body is also a powerful machine. Like a car, your body needs fuel. It gets that fuel from the things you eat and drink. Your body has to digest, or break down, the things you eat and drink so that it can make use of them. Your body needs the nutrients from food to grow and be strong. One of these nutrients is called protein. Protein builds up muscle tissue. Its builds up a healthy body.

Unlike a car, your body comes equipped with a built-in driver: the brain. The brain drives your body all day and all night. It tells your body to do all the things that keep you alive. It tells your heart how fast to pump and your lungs how deep to breathe. It tells your eyes to see and your ears to hear. It tells your body how to be healthy.

The brain also directs the way you grow. One of the many ways the brain does this is by controlling how your body uses the nutrients you get from food. The brain makes certain that your body is using nutrients in the best possible way.

Nutrients are broken down by the body so that they can be passed into the bloodstream and used by the body's cells. Protein is broken down into even smaller units called amino acids. These amino acids are the basic building blocks of a healthy body. They build up healthy body tissues. They build up strong muscles.

How does the brain control the way we use nutrients?

Chemicals in our body called hormones control the way our cells use the nutrients in our food. The brain controls the parts of the body, called glands, that release these chemicals. It tells the glands when to release a hormone and how much of each hormone to release. The brain keeps a very careful measurement of these chemicals. It makes sure that the body has the right amount of each hormone.

There are many different hormones, and they help you grow in different ways. One group of hormones, the male and female hormones, is especially important. They help you to go through the many changes that must happen to make you a healthy adult man or woman.

The hormones that make you a male or female are made in the sex glands (the testicles in males and the ovaries in females). The male hormone is called testosterone; the female hormones are estrogen and progesterone. Testosterone causes a boy's voice to deepen and makes his body and facial hair begin to grow. The female hormones cause a girl's body shape to change, and they make it possible for her to have a baby.

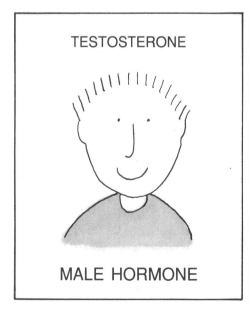

TESTOSTERONE

MALE HORMONE

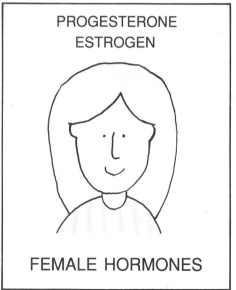

PROGESTERONE
ESTROGEN

FEMALE HORMONES

The bodies of all men and women need a certain amount of both male and female hormones. The body measures these hormones carefully. A man produces more male hormones than female hormones. And a woman produces more female hormones than male hormones. This balancing act makes each of us either a man or a woman. If a person's body produces too much or too little of any one hormone, the body may not grow normally.

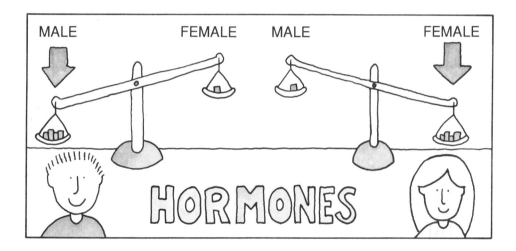

Male and female hormones belong to a special group of hormones called steroids. But male and female hormones are not the only kinds of steroids in the body. Other kinds of steroids are produced in the adrenal glands. These steroids are called corticosteroids. They help the body adjust to stress, fight certain sicknesses, and recover from physical injuries.

The steroids produced by the body are natural steroids. But steroids can also be made in a laboratory. They are called synthetic steroids. Some synthetic steroids are made as pills or capsules; others are made as liquids that are injected into the body with a hypodermic needle.

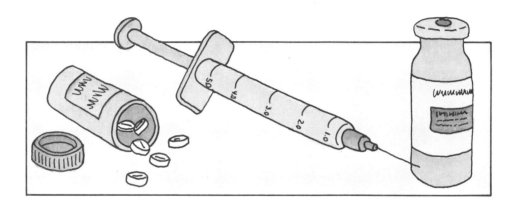

Why would scientists want to make synthetic hormones?

A healthy body produces just the right amount of steroids on its own. But some bodies don't produce enough. Other bodies, either injured or sick, need extra amounts of certain steroids to get healthy again. Therefore, doctors have used both the corticosteroids and the male and female steroids as medicines. They have tried to help those bodies that do not produce enough steroids on their own. They have tried to help those bodies that have illnesses or conditions that can be improved by an additional dose of steroids.

When doctors first used steroids as medicines, they had to get them from the bodies of dead people. This meant that steroids were difficult to get and very expensive. But in the 1930s, scientists learned how to make steroids in a laboratory. These synthetic steroids seemed to work just as well as the body's natural hormones.

Today, doctors use synthetic steroids to treat a variety of medical conditions. Some corticosteroids, such as prednisone and cortisone, are often used to reduce swelling. Doctors have learned that extra amounts of these steroids can help people suffering from arthritis, a painful swelling of the body's joints, and in the treatment of knee and shoulder injuries. Synthetic corticosteroids are also used to fight certain skin diseases and allergies. These steroids are now widely used medicines.

Scientists have also learned how to make synthetic male and female hormones. Anabolic steroids are synthetic male hormones. They are synthetic testosterone, the natural male hormone. The adjective "anabolic" means "tissue-building." These steroids are used by the body to build up muscle tissue.

Anabolic = Tissue-Building

Many years ago, doctors used natural male hormones as medicine to help people whose bodies were weak and frail. When synthetic male hormones were first developed, doctors thought they would have important medical uses. They found that anabolic steroids helped people who were not able to absorb nutrients properly. These people were not able to get enough protein from the things they ate and drank. Doctors treated these patients by giving them high-protein foods and anabolic steroids. The steroids helped them to make better use of the nutrients in food.

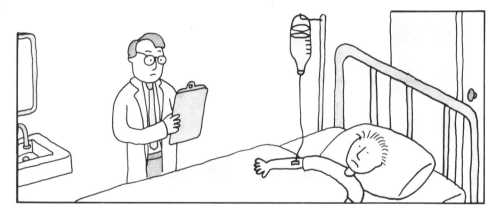

But doctors learned that anabolic steroids had dangerous side effects. They found safer ways to treat medical problems.

It may surprise you to learn that anabolic steroids can be so dangerous. After all, they are very similar to a steroid that the body makes by itself. Why would the body make something that might hurt it? It doesn't seem to make sense.

It's a question of amount.

A plant needs water to survive. Yet too much rain on a corn field can wash the plants away. It's a question of amount.

A plant needs sunshine to survive. Yet too many days of scorching sun will make the plants wither and die. Again, it's a question of amount.

Remember the facts about hormones and a healthy body. The body makes just the right amount of hormones to keep it running smoothly. A person can upset the balance, though, by adding more of any hormone. Then, a person's health can be in danger.

It's a question of amount. And in the case of anabolic steroids, it can be a dangerous and even deadly question.

What Anabolic Steroids Do

Anabolic steroids help the body build up muscles. But they do many other things to the body as well.

Anabolic steroids are synthetic testosterone, the body's natural male hormone. So they produce the same kinds of physical changes that natural testosterone does. They give a young boy the features of a man.

The flow of the natural male hormone is controlled by the brain. But the flow of synthetic testosterone is not. It produces physical changes in a way that is out of control.

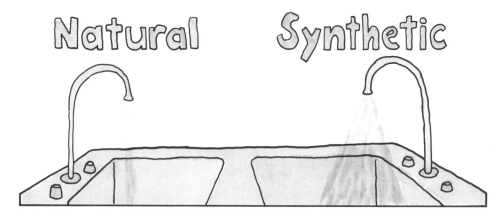

Doctors have reported seeing thick, shaggy hair growth on the arms and legs of some steroid users. Steroid users may also develop heavy cases of pimples. They may even go bald.

These changes are bad enough. But using steroids can cause even more dangerous changes.

Although anabolic steroids are similar to real testosterone, they cannot replace it entirely. The body continues to need a supply of the natural male hormone. But if the body gets doses of synthetic steroids, it may stop producing testosterone. The body no longer has the supply of natural testosterone that it is supposed to have. However, it still has its natural supply of female hormones. The body's natural hormone supply is out of balance.

This often means that the male steroid user loses some of the physical signs of his "maleness." It might mean that a man's breasts will grow and start to resemble female breasts. Some surgeons have even reported performing mastectomies (or breast removal operations) on young men who have used anabolic steroids.

Another change in male steroid users is that the testicles, the sex glands that produce both testosterone and sperm (or reproductive) cells, may become very small. The testicles may never function normally again, even after the use of steroids is stopped. This means that male steroid users may never be able to father children.

Women and Steroids

Because anabolic steroids upset the natural balance of the body's male and female hormones, women who use them are just as much at risk as men are.

It may seem strange that women would want to take doses of a male hormone. But like male athletes, female athletes sometimes use steroids to build stronger muscles. They may get their wish, but like men who use steroids, they pay a price. The price is damage, often permanent damage, to the body.

Every woman has a small supply of testosterone, the male hormone, in her body. But women who take steroids are giving their bodies more testosterone. So they have more male hormones than women normally have. They may lose the physical signs of "femaleness." Their voices become deeper. Their breasts get smaller. They may grow thick, coarse hair on their faces, arms, and shoulders. They may begin to go bald. And they may lose the ability to have babies.

Like male steroid users, women who use steroids run the risk of heart disease, liver disorders, and cancer. It's a big risk for big muscles.

Anabolic steroids can cause heart damage, too. The drugs increase the amount of fats in the blood. This can cause the blood vessels to become clogged and may lead to high blood pressure, strokes, and heart attacks. In fact, heart disease is the leading cause of death among steroid users.

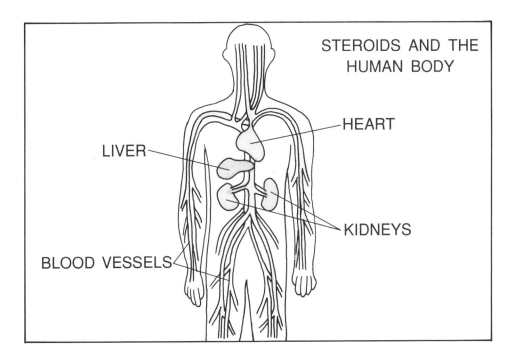

The liver and kidneys often suffer as well. Steroid users may develop blood-filled growths in the liver. Cancer of the liver is the second leading cause of death related to steroid use. Other steroid users have suffered permanent damage to the kidneys.

Anabolic steroids hurt young people even more than they hurt adults. The bodies of young people are still growing, but steroids interfere with the way the body normally develops. They can stop the bones of a young person from growing the way they should. They can stunt a young person's growth. Many teenagers who use steroids remain short for the rest of their lives.

Anabolic steroids do more than damage the body. Like many other drugs, steroids change the way a person thinks, feels, and acts. They change the way the brain works.

Steroids give some people a sense of power and strength, a feeling of vigor and determination. Steroid users say that the drugs give them a "fighting edge." But it is hard to keep this feeling under control. Too often, this "fighting edge" leads to anger and violent behavior. The brain gets out of control.

"Roid Rage"

Many steroid users have been known to fly into angry outbursts for no reason. There have been so many cases of violence brought about by steroid use that the anger has gotten its own name. It's called "roid rage."

Tommy was a college athlete who used steroids. He described what a "roid rage" was like. This is how he felt and reacted when a man accidentally bumped into him:

> "I saw red. I felt an aggression I'd never felt before. I hit him so hard that he went right to the floor. I got him in a headlock and started hitting him in the ribs. I started kneeing him in the back. I wanted to hurt him real bad. I could literally feel the hair standing up on the back of my neck, like I was a wolf or something. If I hadn't been on steroids, I would have walked away in the first place. But I had that cocky attitude. I wanted to try out my new size. It was a test of manhood between two people: you or me, all the way. I was beginning to feel like a killer."

Steroids can cause other effects on the minds of people who use them. Many people who use steroids report that they have trouble getting to sleep; some have terrible nightmares when they do sleep. Some users hear voices that don't exist. Others feel a constant, nagging feeling that people are "out to get them." Still others get a feeling of great importance. One man was convinced that his mind was controlling the events on a television program. He flew into a rage when the story didn't turn out the way he wanted it to.

Other effects on the mind happen when steroid users try to stop using these drugs. Many steroid users report that they become very depressed. Some people even think about killing themselves. One user said, "I don't care if I die as long as I look big in the coffin."

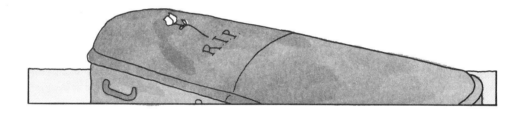

Many users find out that they can't stop using steroids. "I couldn't stop," said one weight lifter about steroids. "Before I started using steroids, I was lifting 250 pounds. I wanted to lift 300. I thought I'd be happy. But then I wanted to lift 400. I kept taking more and more steroids. I just couldn't stop."

Permanent changes, permanent harm, early death: it's a bad bargain made for big muscles. There is even a drawback to the "benefits" of anabolic steroids. Although the damage to the body is often permanent, the "benefits" are not. Once a steroid user stops taking the drug, the muscles shrink back to their normal size. This is one reason why many steroid users keep on taking these drugs, even after they get sick from them. They don't want to lose their muscles. They don't want to lose their strength. They can't let go of their "fighting edge."

It's a bad bargain.

It's a bad bargain that people have been making since steroids were first discovered in the 1930s.

And it's a bad bargain that too many people continue to make today.

The History of Steroids

Anabolic steroids were first created in a laboratory in the 1930s. At first, they were considered "wonder drugs." Doctors thought that these new synthetic drugs would be medicines of great help to the world.

Steroids were used as medicine to help people suffering from starvation and malnutrition. These drugs had two major benefits. First, they enabled the body to use amino acids to build up muscle tissue. Second, the drugs gave many patients a "fighting edge": steroids strengthened their spirit to fight for life.

It was not long before the "fighting edge" that steroids give people was used in other ways. During World War II, Adolf Hitler, the ruler of Germany, ordered that steroids be given to his soldiers. He felt that the drugs would make his soldiers stronger and more violent. It would give them the "fighting edge" they needed to win the war. He wanted to make his soldiers fight as hard as they could, no matter what the cost.

Because of their ability to build up the body and create a "fighting" spirit, anabolic steroids soon entered the world of sports.

In the 1950s, team doctors in the Soviet Union and Eastern Europe began giving anabolic steroids to weight lifters. When combined with a high-protein diet and strenuous training, the steroids allowed the athletes to perform better. Quickly, they began to claim most of the top medals at world weightlifting championships. At the 1952 Olympic games in Finland, the Soviet team won seven medals. This was a tremendous show of strength! Soon, other athletes from the Soviet Union and Eastern Europe began to use the drugs, too.

Many people thought that these athletes must be doing something unfair. But, at that time, there was no way to know whether or not an athlete was using drugs. So the steroids secret was safe. Then, in 1956, an American doctor, John B. Ziegler, went to Austria with the American weightlifting team for an international meet. As an expert in sports medicine, Dr. Ziegler had worked with many American weightlifting teams. Through this work, he became friendly with a Soviet team doctor. At the Austrian meet, the Soviet doctor told Ziegler that his team members were taking injections of testosterone, the male hormone.

The steroids secret was out.

Dr. Ziegler thought that the Soviets now had an unfair advantage over the athletes from other countries. He felt that everyone should be able to share the secret of steroids. When he returned to the United States, he reported what he had learned to the heads of the American athletic committees. But he did more than that. He worked with a drug company to produce anabolic steroids in the United States. At that time, he had no idea that these drugs could be dangerous. He even took them himself to test their safety. When his early tests seemed to show that these drugs worked well and were safe, he gave small doses of them to the weight lifters on his team.

Now, he felt, everyone could benefit from these "wonder drugs." No country would have an unfair advantage.

Years later, Ziegler deeply regretted what he had done. Just before his death in 1984, he said that what started as a "miracle drug" became "one big mess." Over the years, the dangerous effects of anabolic steroids had come to light.

Ziegler took watchful care of his athletes. He gave them very low doses of steroids. He examined them thoroughly for any side effects. The problem was that the steroids worked. They worked too well. His athletes were able to work harder and train longer. They loved the "benefits" of these drugs.

And they started taking more and more of them on their own. "The men went crazy about steroids," Ziegler reported. "They figured if one pill was good, then three or four of them would be better. They were eating them like candy." And it was not just the American weightlifting team. Now that the secret of steroids was out, athletes in other sports and in many other countries began to use them.

At first, athletes were able to get steroids legally. They could get them from team doctors. But as the health dangers of steroid use became better known, many doctors stopped prescribing them for athletes. And, in many states, laws were passed restricting the use of steroids.

Yet the demand for steroids continued to grow. Athletes were soon buying anabolic steroids from drug dealers. By the 1960s, a network of drug dealers, sometimes called a "black market," was making illegal steroids available to anyone who wanted them. Today, drug dealers make over $100 million a year selling steroids in the United States.

The secret was, indeed, out. And so was the beginning of the widespread use of steroids.

Now, anyone who was willing to do *anything* to win had a "miracle drug" to take. Now, young people who would do *anything* to look big and strong had a chemical short cut.

There is no one reason why people use steroids. We know the kinds of pressures that often lead athletes to take such a big risk. We know about the pressure to win.

And we also know the kinds of pressures that lead some young people to try such dangerous drugs. We know about the pressure to grow up.

The Pressure to Grow Up

He knew he was taking a risk. But it didn't matter. He took steroids because he wanted to look big and strong. He thought steroids would make him popular. He thought steroids would help him get a girlfriend.

He got his wish. He even became a defensive tackle on the school football team. One night in October, he played the game of his life. He made four tackles and recovered a fumble. He led his team to a 21-6 victory.

Three days later, he collapsed at football practice. He was taken to a hospital. He died that night. The doctors said that he'd had a heart attack brought on by anabolic steroids. He was 17 years old.

This is the story of one boy who used steroids. It is a true story. And unless young people get the facts about steroids, it is a story that you will hear again and again.

The bodies of young people are always growing, always changing. Some changes are easy for you to see. For example, you know how fast your feet are growing because you keep outgrowing your shoes. Last year's jacket probably doesn't fit anymore, either. And take a look at last year's school picture. You've really changed!

As boys and girls approach the teenage years, their bodies begin to change, inside as well as outside. A boy begins to develop his adult features. His voice deepens. His muscles grow. His body hair gets darker and thicker. He is becoming a man. A girl's body changes, too. She begins to develop her adult body shape. Her breasts grow. Her hips develop. She is becoming a woman.

These changes happen because the bodies of boys and girls begin to create more male and female hormones. The bodies of all boys and girls produce some of each hormone. But only boys have testicles, which produce large amounts of testosterone, and only girls have ovaries, which produce large amounts of estrogen and progesterone. It's these sex glands that determine the amount of male and female hormones in the body.

The time during which a child begins to turn into an adult is called adolescence. It can often be a difficult and confusing time. Adolescence often seems to begin overnight. So many changes start to happen! And sometimes it seems that they all happen at once. Some teenagers have growth spurts, when the body changes rapidly. Others have sudden mood swings. One minute a teenager may feel happy and proud. The next minute he or she may feel discouraged or depressed.

Such quick changes can be very unsettling, even scary. They occur because the body is trying to manage a new flow of hormones. Somewhere deep in the body, it is almost as though a faucet of hormones has been turned on.

Not all teenagers change quickly. For some, changes seem to take a long time. They may see their friends growing more quickly. They may wait and wait to see those changes begin in themselves. For many young people, slow changes can be unsettling and scary, too.

And sometimes boys and girls want to hurry the growing process along. They look for a short cut.

Why do some young people want to grow up in a hurry?

One part of the answer is peer pressure. Peer pressure is the feeling that you have to do something because other people your own age are doing it. Peer pressure means doing something to "fit in" with other kids. It means doing something to be one of the crowd.

Everyone wants to be popular. It's only natural to want to be liked by other kids. It's only natural to want to be like other kids. But what happens when we feel pressure to do something we would rather not do? What happens when we feel pressure to do something we think is wrong?

Can you say "No" to peer pressure when you want to?

Most kids can. But for some kids, the pressure to grow up and the pressure to fit in lead to trouble. For some kids, these pressures can lead to drugs. Other kids turn to drugs because they think drugs will help them to feel better when they are sad or discouraged. They may think that using drugs is a way to forget the problems and pressures of growing up.

There is another kind of pressure in adolescence. During the teenage years, boys and girls become more aware of each other. They are attracted to each other in new ways. They have their first feelings of love. A boy who is interested in a girl wants to look good in her eyes. And a girl wants to be attractive to the boy she's interested in, too.

These feelings of wanting to look good create pressure. The pressure is increased by what's going on inside the body. If a girl looks at her body and sees only a child, she may feel unattractive. If a boy's body isn't developing as quickly as he would like it to, he may feel weak and unattractive, too.

Michael's Story

Some teenage boys use anabolic steroids to "speed up" their growth. When growing up seems to be taking too long, a young boy may be tempted to try a chemical short cut. He may be tempted to try steroids.

But boys who use anabolic steroids to look more grown-up take a terrible risk. Michael took that risk.

At the age of 15, Michael felt skinny and weak compared to other boys. His classmates picked on him and teased him because he was small. He began to work out every day with a set of weights. He built up his muscles so that at age 16, he was 5' 9" and weighed 165 pounds.

But Michael wasn't satisfied. He wanted to be even bigger. That's when he discovered anabolic steroids. He bought some illegally at a local gym. Soon he was up to 193 pounds. But Michael began to have violent mood swings. He would fly into anger over little things. His grades began to slip. His family and friends noticed that he was often deeply depressed.

At the age of 17, Michael shot himself in the head with a rifle and died.

His sister said, "Steroids pulled the trigger."

Everybody is different. Everybody grows at his or her own pace. For some young people, the changes of adolescence seem to creep along slowly. For others, the changes seem to happen overnight. Each body has its own natural rhythm of growth. Each body has its own built-in clock.

Using anabolic steroids disrupts this natural growth pace. A wildly ticking clock takes the place of the body's built-in clock. Using anabolic steroids leads to an unnatural and stressful pace of growth. The body is already under stress during adolescence, trying to manage its own new flow of hormones. But when someone uses steroids, the body suddenly has to cope with a *flood* of hormones that it just can't manage.

Young people are not the only ones who feel the pressure to fit in. Adults feel peer pressure, too. They have to be strong enough to say "No" to peer pressure, too.

Like most kids, most adults do say "No." Most adults are strong enough to say "No" to the wrong kinds of pressure. But like some kids, some adults do give in. They give in to the pressure to use drugs.

Steroids and Sports

In three different surveys, groups of athletes were asked: "Would you take a pill that would help you to win a gold medal, but that would kill you within one year?"

More than half of the athletes answered, "Yes."

Sports are supposed to be fun. But sometimes the fun gets lost in the drive to win. One Olympic coach compared the world of sports to war: "Competition is just like a war. We do what we have to do to win the war." What do they have to do to win the war? Some people want to win so much that they are willing to do anything. They are willing to use drugs.

How widespread is the use of steroids among athletes?

The use of steroids can be found almost everywhere in sports today. High-school and college athletes are using them. Professional athletes are using them, too. Surveys show that between 70% and 90% of all professional football players have used steroids.

And Ben Johnson was not alone when he used them at the 1988 Olympics. It has been estimated that more than half of the 9,000 Olympic athletes were using steroids.

Why?

Why do athletes want to use steroids?

Because steroids work.

Dr. Robert Cantu is an expert in sports medicine and a medical consultant to the United States Olympic Boxing Team. He knows that steroids work. He knows that the problem with steroids is that they work so well:

> *"Weight lifters can do the maximum lifts only every other week. On steroids, they can do those lifts every week. So the person who would be stiff and sore and really beat up for days after the maximum lifts suddenly isn't. The amount of training, the quality of the training, and the determined attitude to keep training—these are all much greater if the person is using steroids. That's the tragedy: steroids work."*

"Give Me What It Takes"

Athletes know that steroids work. They know that anabolic steroids can make their muscles grow. They know that weight gain can be quick and dramatic. They know that steroids can help them to work out harder and longer.

Of course, many of them know the risks of taking steroids, too. But often they don't care. This is how one athlete described his experience with steroids:

> *"People who tell you steroids don't work don't know what they're talking about. You can work out much harder than before, and your muscles don't get as sore. You're more motivated in the weight room. You've got lots more energy. But besides the muscle growth, there were other things happening to me. I got real bad acne on my back. My hair started to come out. I was having trouble sleeping. And my testicles began to shrink. All the side effects you hear about. But it didn't matter. My mind was set. I didn't care about that other stuff. My attitude was: just give me what it takes to be big."*

Some athletes think that they have to use steroids to compete with other athletes who are using these drugs. They want to "even the score." They think that they have to use steroids to win. Olga Fikotova Connolly was a track and field champion. She won the gold medal for discus throwing at the 1956 Olympic games. She competed in five Olympics. And she did it without using drugs. But she knows that things are different today: "There is no way in the world a woman nowadays can break the world record in the throwing events unless she is using steroids. These awful drugs have changed everything."

Birgit Dressel was a champion track star from West Germany. Her event was the heptathlon, a difficult seven-part track and field event. She won fourth place in the 1986 European Athletic Championships. In 1987, she was ranked sixth in the world. She hoped to win a gold medal at the 1988 Olympics. But in April 1987, following a regular practice session, she felt a stabbing pain in her lower back. She was rushed to the hospital, but it was too late. Steroids had already destroyed her kidneys and liver. That night, Dressel died at the age of 26.

The message about steroids is clear. Today, steroid use is not permitted in many athletic competitions. More and more athletes are being tested to be certain that they are not using steroids. There are new, drug-free competitions open only to athletes who don't use steroids. But no matter how clear the message might be, too many athletes continue to use these dangerous drugs.

Why would athletes use a drug they know is dangerous?

Because they want to win. Because they want to win more than anything. Because they are willing to do anything to win.

> Winning is a matter of pride. We want to do our best at whatever we do. Sometimes, though, we put our pride before everything else.
>
> Here's how one athlete did just that:
>
> *"The coaches wanted us to be as aggressive as possible, and it didn't matter where that aggression came from. The coaches got me to respond by going after my pride. If they said I was a bum, I had to prove I wasn't. So I decided to take steroids to get big and strong and aggressive. I didn't care if I died, as long as I completed the season, as long as I finished like a man."*

Many top-level athletes feel that they can't afford to come in second. To them, being second-best means the same thing as losing. Winning means so much that many steroid users can't stop using the drugs, even when they know that steroids are making them sick. The pressure to win is too strong.

The pressure to win is not just on the athletes. Coaches, trainers, and even team doctors also know about the pressure to win. In fact, some feel the pressure so much that they have encouraged their players to take steroids.

This is how two athletes described the pressure they felt to use anabolic steroids:

"We had to take steroids. They told us to take them."

"Steroids were just given to us, like vitamin pills."

And this is what Ben Johnson says happened to him.

Ben Johnson says that his coach and team physician let him take steroids. Johnson says they never told him about the health risks. He trusted their judgment.

Ben Johnson felt tremendous pressure to win. He wanted to win for the glory of winning. He wanted to win for the chance to set a new world record. He wanted to be the fastest man alive.

He wanted to be the best.

There was another reason Ben Johnson wanted to win. Olympic champions often win more than medals. Ben Johnson had been offered a $2.8-million contract with a company that makes sports clothing. If he won the Olympic race, he would be paid to appear in their ads. The gold that Ben Johnson was running for was not just the gold medal. Winning that race meant earning a great deal of money.

Today, sports is a big business. Famous athletes can make a lot of money by doing advertisements. You've seen athletes doing ads for cereals, soft drinks, and clothing. You've seen their names on baseball bats, tennis racquets, and footballs. But if they weren't champions, they would never be offered such deals. They wouldn't make so much money. The deals and the money are part of the prize they get for being winners.

Team coaches and trainers are under enormous pressure to win. And some cheat by encouraging their athletes to use drugs. But when they do, they are cheating the very people they are supposed to be helping.

Young people with dreams of being athletic champions are also under enormous pressure to win. And some cheat by using drugs. But when they do, they are cheating themselves.

What does Ben Johnson have to say? Speaking before the United States Congress on October 5, 1989, he said, "I got caught and lost my gold medal. I'm here to tell people that it's wrong to cheat. Don't take drugs. They're bad for your health. I was lucky: I got caught."

Ben Johnson took steroids, and they hurt him. They hurt his body. Johnson's liver may be permanently damaged. They also hurt his athletic career. Johnson hopes to be a top racer again. His two-year suspension ended September 1990. But it may be hard for him to compete after such a long layoff. He may never get to be the best he could be. He may never get to show what he could have done—without drugs.

But, now, Johnson has a chance to let people, especially young people, know the facts about steroids. Now, he can keep steroids from hurting other people, too.

Maybe Ben Johnson really *is* lucky.

An Interview with a Former Steroid User

Ralph is a competitive body builder. He started seriously training in 1982. Soon after that, he began to use steroids.

How and why did you first use steroids?

I was 24 years old. I wanted to be a professional body builder. But I just couldn't get my weight above 213 pounds. That's when another body builder told me about steroids. He said they would put on the weight I wanted—and they did. Fast. In six months, I was up to 257. I thought that steroids were safe, and I started out at a low dose—three pills a day. After a while, I began to take more. My body got big, lean, and hard. Everybody else in body building was taking them. I just thought it was something I *had* to do.

They made me more impatient. I'd get angry very easily, especially when I was driving my car. If I had to stop for a red light, I'd get very upset. I felt rushed, always in a hurry, kind of "on edge" all the time. I also had trouble sleeping at night. My blood pressure went way up, too. I started to lose my hair. And I got some fatty tumors on my body.

I was *always* frightened. But not enough to stop. The competition was so tough. I looked around the gym, and the guys who were at the weight I wanted to be at were all using steroids.

I kept telling myself that every profession had risks. Telling myself that helped me to avoid looking at the risks I was facing, I guess. I was fooling myself, but it worked.

I thought nothing would really happen to me. Not to me.

So that's how I talked myself into using steroids.

> *Did you ever get sick or injured because of steroids?*

Yes, I had a bad injury, and that's why I finally stopped using them. I was at a championship powerlifting meet. In powerlifting, there are three events—bench press, squat, and dead lift. I had deadlifted 675 pounds pretty regularly in practice. But at this meet, I wanted to go for 700. You get so pumped up, you know? Steroids make you feel that you can do anything. So I did lift 700 pounds, but I felt something pop inside the top of my left arm. It felt like a rubber band snapping. I heard a sound like a big rip. My tendon had snapped. My bicep just bunched all up. It rolled up my arm, like a window shade.

I went to the emergency room of the hospital. There, the doctor said that the muscle, some nerves, and even some bone tissue had separated from the large bone in my arm. The doctors had to operate. They carved out a ditch in the big bone and put the tendon in there. Then, they drilled two holes in the bone and threaded the tendon through to the other side of my bone. They had to anchor it down by my elbow. It was really painful.

> ### *Can you use your arm fully today?*

It will never be the way it should be. It scared me, you know? It made me think that steroids weren't so great. I don't drink. I don't smoke. I'm an athlete. So I always felt a real conflict about using steroids. It was hard for me to admit that I was a drug user. I was hurting my body. I was taking drugs.

> ### *When did you stop using steroids?*

In 1987. I had used steroids for about three years. I stopped after the injury. I began to rethink things. I began to see that my whole life was centered around a goal that was too risky. I saw that I didn't have much else going for me, that my life was being *run* by powerlifting and body building. I didn't know the real me. Any drug that keeps you from knowing who you are, deep inside, is bad. I needed some time out to figure out who I was. Then, to be honest with you, once I stopped using steroids, I liked the way I felt so much that I knew I'd never go back. I made peace with myself. Today, I feel a freedom I didn't before. I don't need steroids to feel good about myself.

> *What advice do you have for young athletes*
> *who may be tempted to take steroids?*

I have seen drug-free powerlifters go really far. They're successful, and they have healthy bodies and good lives. And, today, there are many more drug-free competitions. Athletes *can* succeed without drugs. And, without drugs, they can also have better and fuller lives. People who live their lives with only one goal—to be a great professional athlete, for example—often don't end up being happy people, I think. I'd urge young people to put balance in their lives. Be a great athlete if you can. But don't forget about other things in your life. Be a friend, too. Be a well-rounded person. There's more to life than winning a game, you know? It's very important to remember that.

Drug-Free Winners

John Ziegler, the man who introduced anabolic steroids to America, wished that he hadn't. If he could have turned back the clock to 1956, he probably would have destroyed his "miracle drug."

But history is history. It can't be changed.

Ben Johnson would probably like another chance, too. A chance to start over—to win, or lose, without drugs.

But, again, history is history. It can't be changed.

What *can* change?

Athletes can make the decision to be drug-free. They can make the choice to be the best they can be. They can do it through talent and teamwork. They can do it through exercise and a healthy diet. They can do it through practice and hard work. And they can do it without drugs.

Young people can make the decision to be drug-free. They can decide that what's inside a person is what counts. They can decide that it takes more than muscles to be a winner.

Who can make that change happen?

You! *You* can make the decision to be drug-free. You and your friends can!

You are now developing winning skills. On and off the athletic field, you are beginning to find your place. You're beginning to build your talents. You can do it on your own. You can be a real winner. You can do it by saying "No" to cheating. You can do it by saying "No" to dangerous short cuts. You can do it by saying "No" to drugs.

A Happy Ending

By the time he was 17, Aaron had taken steroids for five years. He was a star on his high-school football team. But Aaron had terrible health problems. He often flew into violent rages or went into deep depressions. He couldn't stop taking the drugs, though.

One night, Aaron gave up. He swallowed a whole bottle of medicine, trying to end his life. He was rushed to the hospital. Aaron did not die that night. Instead, he took the first step on the road toward a new life.

Medical tests showed that steroid use had caused damage to his liver, kidneys, and stomach. A doctor warned him, "If you don't quit steroids, you'll die."

This time, Aaron did stop. Now, at the age of 20, he works hard to warn other young people about the risks of steroid use. Here are Aaron's words, taken from a talk he gave at his own high school:

"I took steroids because I didn't believe in myself. I learned the hard way that what matters is how you feel about yourself, not what people think about you. What others think fades away, but what you feel inside lasts as long as you live."

Believe in yourself. Say "No" to steroids.

On and off the playing field, you want to be a winner. Breaking records and winning races are important. So is the feeling of "being the best" or of "looking like a champ." But there are things of far greater value than a gold medal or a Superman image.

A healthy, happy, and drug-free life is one of them.

There are so many things to say "Yes" to. Say "Yes" to working hard to practice your skills. Say "Yes" to growing up safely. Say "Yes" to feeling good inside.

Someday you might even get to say "Yes" when you are offered an Olympic gold medal!

But whatever you do, win or lose, you will know that you have done it on your own. You will deserve the pride you feel. You will be a drug-free winner! And that's the only real kind of winner there is.

Glossary

adolescence   the stage of life when a child begins to turn into an adult

adrenal glands   the glands that produce corticosteroids

amino acids   a chemical substance that is the basic building block of protein

anabolic   a term that means "tissue building"; *see: anabolic steroids*

anabolic steroids   a group of synthetic male hormones; often used to build a more muscular body

"black market"   an illegal network of drug dealers and buyers

corticosteroids   a group of hormones produced by the adrenal glands; often used as medicine

cortisone   one of several synthetic corticosteroids

dealer   a person who sells illegal drugs

estrogen   a female sex hormone

"fighting edge"   a feeling of strength and determination brought about by anabolic steroids

gland   an organ that produces hormones

hormone	a chemical substance that controls a function or process of the human body
natural steroids	steroids that are produced by the body
ovaries	female sex glands that produce the hormones estrogen and progesterone
peer pressure	the feeling that you have to do something because other people your age are doing it
prednisone	one of several synthetic corticosteroids
progesterone	a female sex hormone
protein	a nutrient, made up of amino acids, needed to build and repair body tissue
"roid rage"	violent behavior brought about by the use of anabolic steroids
sex glands	the glands that produce the sex hormones; (testicles in males, ovaries in females)
steroids	a group of hormones that includes anabolic steroids and corticosteroids
synthetic steroids	steroids that are made in a laboratory
testicles	male sex glands that produce the hormone testosterone
testosterone	the male sex hormone

Index